T0273056

BLACK QUEER HOE

The BreakBeat Poets series

The BreakBeat Poets series, curated by Kevin Coval and Nate Marshall, is committed to work that brings the aesthetic of hip-hop practice to the page. These books are a cipher for the fresh, with an eye always to the next. We strive to center and showcase some of the most exciting voices in literature, art, and culture.

BreakBeat Poets series titles include:

The BreakBeat Poets: New American Poetry in the Age of Hip-Hop,
edited by Kevin Coval, Quraysh Ali Lansana, and Nate Marshall

This Is Modern Art: A Play, Idris Goodwin and Kevin Coval

The BreakBeat Poets Vol. 2: Black Girl Magic, edited by Mahogany L. Browne, Jamila Woods, and Idrissa Simmonds

Human Highlight, Idris Goodwin and Kevin Coval

On My Way to Liberation, H. Melt

Citizen Illegal, José Olivarez

Graphite, Patricia Frazier

The BreakBeat Poets Vol. 3: Halal if You Hear Me,
edited by Fatimah Asghar and Safia Elhillo

There are Trans People Here, H. Melt

Commando, E'mon Lauren

BLACK QUEER HOE

Britteney Black Rose Kapri

Foreword by Danez Smith

Published in 2018 by
Haymarket Books
P.O. Box 180165
Chicago, IL 60618
773-583-7884
www.haymarketbooks.org
info@haymarketbooks.org

ISBN: 978-1-60846-952-9

Trade distribution:
In the US, Consortium Book Sales and Distribution, www.cbsd.com
In Canada, Publishers Group Canada, www.pgcbooks.ca
In the UK, Turnaround Publisher Services, www.turnaround-uk.com
All other countries, Ingram Publisher Services International,
IPS_Intlsales@ingramcontent.com

This book was published with the generous support of Lannan Foundation and Wallace Action Fund.

Entered into digital printing October, 2019.

Cover design by Rachel Cohen. Cover photograph, Nadiyah (2017) by Maya Iman. www.mayaiman.com

Library of Congress Cataloging-in-Publication data is available.

Go Go Gadget Hoe
@BlkRseKapri

Pro Black. Pro Queer. Pro Hoe.

Translate from Portuguese

5:59 PM · 17 Jan 16

v

contents

Foreword

LOOK AT THIS FAT BITCH

marvel at me. take it all in.
make   me   famous.
ain't no victim here. no shame.
just good lighting
and a fuckable face.
—from "the day my nudes leak"

It is my firm belief and chief recommendation that this book be read out loud in the back corner of the bus huddled up next to one or two of your best niggas; or in the living room, two on the couch and two on the floor, a blunt and a bag of something spicy being passed around; or in your room, alone, something mellow and hood turned all the way up, so loud it's silence. Some of y'all won't have access to some of those ways. This book isn't for y'all and that's okay. Britteney Black Rose Kapri knows the gazes set upon her and in *Black Queer Hoe* she sets the conditions of our looking. From jump, the title tells us the body, in all its shapes and ways, would take center stage. *Black Queer Hoe* is at once a naming, a call for kin, a warning, a prayer too. *Black Queer Hoe* so you don't get it confused. *Black Queer Hoe* so boom. A kind of *what had happened*. The context. The landscape.

Kapri maps a Black femme interior pastoral through poems alive somewhere between monologue and a confession. These highlight a link from the lyric of Lucille Clifton to the stand-up of Sommore as Kapri's speaker slips from comic to storyteller to auntie to testifier. These poems locate themselves in rich Black femme oral traditions of dissing and telling the truth which span from porches to juke joints and main stages, reaching for Clifton's imaginative vulnerability and June Jordan's ferocity in the key of Mo'Nique. These poems teach us about the belly laughs born out of wounds, interrogating and distrusting the same humor they embrace and defend with. The poem "Bitch" begins "i'm the last one catcalled / outta me and my Bitches," gesturing toward a confession before swerving toward humor with "probably cause i got bitch / pheromones." This poem, like many of Kapri's poems, pivots so quickly through complex webs of tone, while patterns lure us into being disarmed. The poem bounces with repetition and litany, tools Kapri leans on often to build her poems that play well with her athletic ability to oscillate tone in a poem. The poem ends:

> men love to love me, i am *that* Bitch.
> men love to love the idea of me
> they don't think i bitch.
>
> men love me until i'm *that* crazy
> bitch. men don't want me
> calling myself a Bitch so they can.
>
> on the wrong tongue queen and Bitch
> sound the same.

Here, Kapri gestures back at the audience, sending any man excusing himself from this poem to examine his own mouth. Many of these poems talk back to several audiences: to men on Twitter, men on trains, people in the speaker's bed, to white women, to family, to friends. The poet uses the address all through the collection both as an extension of love and an act of defense. Everyone gets called out or in, everyone gets shouted out or implicated. Whatever the energy, it's Kapri's time to sound off. This collection is capital-B Black Girl (un)interrupted, unfiltered, sometimes a sermon and sometimes a secret. We move from the large-swath, big personality of Black femininity and queerness to more intimate and lyrical works like "of wanting" and "hidradenitis suppurativa pt. 1," where the speaker's skin condition and possible insecurity is offered as "a soft succulent. a little ugly cactus." These moments reveal a voice underneath the voice, one more intimate and insular, stripped of the bravado and those notes of stand-up. These moments offer us lines that are quieter and a speaker who is less concerned with addressing anyone besides themself or an intimate *you*. Kapri also employs that gentler lyric in the lush "purple" where a purple-skinned character speaks:

> but i hear them, hear them tell their friends i am
> lavender instead of raisin. praise the lilac and periwinkle
> children they forced into me. i see it, the slow erasure
> of my fig, my mulberry. i hear them say *plum plague, plum*
> *magic, plum list, plum mail* and i know that is not an accident.

Oh I want to eat this poem. How beautiful this pain is in Kapri's hands. The surrealist nod of this poem echoes through the collection as forts made out of dicks and erotic poems for blenders; Kapri is just as sharp and tender when trying to make us laugh as when she's trying to let us in. The generosity of this collection comes in how it holds something and how bare Kapri allows us to see her. I hate when white people describe a Black poet's work as "raw," but I wanna say very Blackly that this collection is raw, raw how we said it in 2003 and how niggas from Milwaukee say it today, *raaaaw*—bloody even when graceful, a foul-mouthed book of psalms.

Folks call work "unflinching" too. I don't know if I vibe with that. I think I like work that flinches a little bit, work that addresses fear in a way that some label as fearlessness. To hell with fearlessness. These poems know fear and embrace it; their strength is drawn not from an attempt to vanquish fear but an attempt to understand the matrix of it, to learn to strive beside it. This brazen debut is good medicine and a needed shout in the world. *Black Queer Hoe* makes it clear Britteney Black Rose Kapri is a poet we must pay attention to, taking up the reins of many spoken word and literary ancestors and charging forward into poetics unafraid to be ratchet and bare. Welcome to this motherfucking book! Journey into these poems knowing that Kapri might take care of you but she also might cuss you out. Enter knowing damn well you might get told about yourself as the Black Queer Hoe sings her song.

Danez Smith

Go Go Gadget Hoe
@BlkRseKapri

When niggas call me queen I'm start replying with "of what?"

6:59 PM · 21 May 17 from Chicago, IL

tindr

allow me to reintroduce myself, my name is Britteney
Black Rose Kapri aka Bee aka Besus Fights aka Go Go Gadget
Hoe aka That Bitch Your Mother Wishes You'd Marry (but
you know better). of House Slytherin. first of her name.
Queen of the Clapback. Patron Saint of Fat Bitches with too
much mouth and even more tiddy. Duchess of Depression.
Right Honorable Magistrate of Cellulite and Twerk.
Professor Pop Off. Elder Petty. Admiral of Hoe Tendencies
and Anxiety. Captain Can't Save Em, but i keep trying. Siren
to lost-cause niggas and light-skin rappers. Master of Self
Deprecation. High Priestess of the Pen and Mic. Countess of
Shut a Nigga Down. Server of Shade and These Hands.
Chairman of the Curve. Emperor of Don't Come For Me.
Lord of I Didn't Send for You. Don of the fuck your mixtape,
papa john's, indiana, j. cole, and your misogynistic facebook
statuses. Mother of Draggings.

all these poets is my sons. i create space for marginalized
youth to counter the narrative being forced upon them.
i also punt toddlers for crying on airplanes. i drink like a
sailor and fuck like my mother. i ain't got time for your
shit, so come correct boy or don't come at all. i chef like
your southern granny and bougie northern auntie that ran
and never looked back. spent the past twenty-nine years
working on being the best version of myself, which means
loving the worst versions of myself. ain't no shrew to be
tamed, ain't no horse to be broke, ain't no Hoe to be
housewived. i be all this and i ain't gone stop. i got my own
house, my own car, work two jobs, imma bad Bitch. But if
you call me Bitch i'll skin you.

reasons imma Hoe

i fucked someone else. i was walking. he asked a question he didn't want the answer to. her man finds me attractive. she doesn't find herself attractive. the internet. a woman in church didn't like that i walked like a grown woman. i was switching. i grew hips too young. my friends. i got on the wrong train car. i grew breasts too young. i distracted the boys from their schoolwork by showing my shoulders. by showing my thighs. by showing up. i loved a woman. i touched a woman. i left a woman. i fucked more people than him. he didn't teach me that thing he liked. i didn't like that thing he likes. i didn't wait for him. i didn't smile for him. i smiled at another him. i carried condoms. i let him fuck me without a condom. i said no. i said yes. i spoke. i didn't bleed. i did exactly what he asked me to. i told him that shit was weird. i blocked him. i fucked her man. i was breathing.

zaddy

he bends me over and asks me to call him daddy so i say
who? or blocked number. or yeah, i understand, next time.
you say i have daddy issues. so, it's tuesday and i still want
to be loved. and sometimes love is a call two days after
your birthday with a promise you know can't be kept. but
it feels good that he's still trying. that you've learned to
wrap yourself in his good intentions and lull yourself to
sleep. i keep telling myself i don't want men anything like
my father but the last four dudes i've taken seriously have
been libras and sometimes they forget to text or show up.
and if that's not a daddy then i don't know what is.

bad feminist

i like it when he tells me to shut up and suck his dick.
when he shoves his whole hand in my mouth. the spanks
before the bruises. when he tells me to call him daddy.

when she shoves my face in the mattress. when he
commands me back into the bed. both her hands wrapped
around my neck. when she asked if it was too hard.

when he made sure i was sure. when she did her research.
when she stopped even though i gave him permission.
when she still said no. when he waited until i was sober.

Go Go Gadget Hoe
@BlkRseKapri

It's 94°.
All praises be Sweet Baby Jamie Lee
Curtis, the Original Scream Queen
cause I love dressing like a hoe.

3:23 PM · 20 Sep 17

shawty with the ass

this one time

this boy say   *ay girl with the ass.*
and all i hear is church bells and little jays pitter-pattering
across the train floor. it's like *i ain't even know i had an ass*
like *what have i been sitting on all these years.*
he say *what you doing* and since we're both on the train
i can tell he's going places so i give him my number.

or

how do i curve this nigga without leaving on a stretcher.
how fresh is my manicure, am i willing to break a nail off in
a nigga. where are the exits. does it look like anyone here
will fight for me. can i walk the rest of the way. will the
cops believe me. will the news use my mug shot.

after a certain hour

i only ride in the first train car, unless it smells like shit. i
never sit with my back to a man if i have a choice. i keep a
knife open in my pocket or a key between my ring and
index finger. i keep headphones in but not too loud. i try to
only sit by Black women. they're the only people i trust
besides myself.

this one time

a man follows me home from the train. forty feet from my
house i face him and start wiping my knife on my jeans. he
walks away. every time i tell that story someone asks what
i would have done if he kept coming.

open letter to the mothers who shield their daughters from looking at me

no ma'am you wouldn't want your daughter to be like me, i sucked dick this morning and didn't brush my teeth. and yes my hat, necklace, and septum ring all say Bitch. and i used to burn myself and lie about it. and i've forgot how many men have forgotten my name but not what i look like bent over. and i curse like a pirate fucked a veteran fucked a barkeep fucked my mom and had me. and i got tattoos in places you didn't even know you could get them. and i touch women in places you warn your daughter to not let boys near. i've pierced some of those places too. sometimes i stand naked in my kitchen. and i sleep with men in relationships. but not married ones that's too much drama. and i feed off of drama like my uncle and a bottle. and i do drugs. drug drugs not pot. and i smoke that too. and i steal from target. imma feminist and i watch punishment porn. and instead of a list of respectable shit i do, all i'll say is i respect my elders. see i called you ma'am when i could've called you bitch.

an incomplete list:
of women i should apologize to

-every woman i met before 2015
-more specifically
-fat girls more confident than me
-slash fat girls
-less confident
-ashley
-any woman i took pictures of
-my first girlfriend
-kiela
-or the next
███████████
-girls i kissed to appease boys
-hoodrats i thought i was better than
-hoodrats i thought i wasn't
-strippers
-girls who wore lace fronts before 2015
-all the women whose boyfriends i fucked
██████████
████████████
████████████████████████
-some of y'all
-are still bitches
-anyone i called a bitch
-which is not the same as
-my bitch
-or
-biiiiiiiiiiiitch

what raych means when she says
Biiiiiiiiiiiiiiiiiitch

reclamation
as in:

-do we need to fight a bitch Bitch
-these niggas got me fucked up
-get your fucking shit together
-i'll be there in thirty minutes
-you know what you did
-what that nigga do now
-let's turn the fuck up
-guess the fuck what
-just one more drink
-i'm sad come over
-i'm running late
-you look good
-who said that
-i love you

before they can use it against you

imma lego-body ass bitch.
square head round peg ass bitch.

no torso, t-rex arms, whole body legs but still 5′2″ ass
bitch. grown with baby teeth ass bitch.

my ass fat but my neck fatter looking ass bitch.
keep my nails long cause my hair won't grow ass bitch.

don't know the words lip-syncing on snapchat ass bitch.
can't see but always watching from the sidelines ass bitch.

got jokes but no friends ass bitch.
call it depression but i'm just being lazy ass bitch.

got seven names but don't answer to any of em ass bitch.
say she queer but can't eat pussy ass bitch.

Go Go Gadget Hoe
@BlkRseKapri

Sia "leaking" her own nudes so someone couldn't sell them is the cornerstone of my feminism.

2:17 PM · 07 Nov 17 from Chicago, IL

Bitch

i'm the last one catcalled
outta me and my Bitches.
probably cause i got bitch
pheromones.

got a bitch back up off me
before i cut you swagger.
my pussy a bitch nigga repellent.
pussy so good

you could get lost in that Bitch.
men love to love me, i am *that* Bitch.
men love to love the idea of me
they don't think i bitch.

men love me until i'm *that* crazy
bitch. men don't want me
calling myself a Bitch so they can.

on the wrong tongue queen and Bitch
sound the same.

real women[1] have

curves
flat asses
dicks
voter registration cards
lace fronts
guns
criminal records
girlfriends
door knocker earrings
children
adam's apples
power suits
a-cups
hormone replacement therapy
dirt under their nails
tucks
only a high school degree
testosterone
infertility
bald heads
breast reductions
names

---

1 stop killing us

Go Go Gadget Hoe
@BlkRseKapri

Harriet Tubman did not die for my sins to deal with y'alls slut shaming/ homophobic bullshit,

6:58 PM · 17 Jan 16

Queer enough

sometimes i think i haven't loved enough women to call
myself Queer. haven't fought off enough dudes trying to
turn me back. haven't been invited cause i am not public
enough. haven't been kicked out of enough. haven't cut
off enough family for speaking out the side of they necks.
haven't ate enough pussy. haven't gone to enough gay
spaces. haven't needed enough gay spaces. haven't
defiantly held enough hands in the face of potential
violence. haven't bled enough. haven't felt out of place
enough. haven't been accused of wandering eyes in the
locker room enough. haven't lost enough friends. though
i've lost enough friends. haven't had enough rumors
spread. haven't been hated enough.

pansexual

yes, i do like pans. and pots. and slow cookers. and woks.
and crock-pots. and rice makers. and panini presses. and
waffle irons. and blenders when i am feeling dangerous.
and juicers. and cold presses. and food processors. and
watercoolers. and espresso makers. and cast-iron skillets.
god damn do i love me a good cast-iron skillet. and
microwaves. and griddles. and plates. and whatever the
fuck my partner wants to call themselves.

to every nigga that told me their dick belonged to me

for kush thompson

i am building a fort with these dicks.
washing em off and regifting these dicks.
i've run out of shelves for these dicks.
got a crown made of the best dicks.
stack three together
and it's a lightsaber dick.

i even recycle the dicks.
reduce, reuse, resuck these dicks.
fortifying a wall around my bed of these dicks.
put on a puppet show starring these dicks.
if i leave one behind got a whole arsenal of these dicks.
i go on antiques roadshow with these dicks.
most time i don't even want these dicks.

to every nigga i ever yelled out "this pussy is yours" to, you welcome

welcome to this prestigious club, niggas who i lied to, niggas whose numbers i never saved, niggas who i loved so fervently i was willing to gift them what others took without asking. do y'all call each other? have a special handshake? take turns reminiscing when you were lucky enough to be face first in this moist cavern of greatness? i hope you didn't think i meant it was *yours* yours, like *just* yours. it's more like a time-share, where you're only allowed to come over between 1 and 6 a.m. only speak to tell me how much you missed being here. one day i might retire, might let someone's daddy or auntie put a ring on it. lock me down until their retirement plan dries out. but then again, who am i to deny this safe haven to the masses? sorry i haven't called in a while. haven't answered your texts, dms, emails, tweets, smoke signals. i've just been so busy being too busy for you. but it's cool, absence makes the pussy taste sweeter.

to the nigga who tweeted
"we need to stop glorifying fat people"
while secretly receiving my nudes
behind his girlfriend's back

nigga please, i made you
call me glory. mouth full of me.
commanded you bow
before this dimpled ass.
pray to the belly
that overhangs this pussy.
give thanks for how bountiful
this body is.

Go Go Gadget Hoe
@BlkRseKapri

"Don't be as fuckboy" - Harriet
Tubman

7:40 AM · 16 Apr 16

Go Go Gadget Hoe
@BlkRseKapri

Take More Nudes.
Trust Less People.

8:28 PM · 30 Jan 17 from Chicago, IL

the day my nudes leak

imma virus-passed
secret. wildfire
burning holes in good
men's browsers.
not your daddy's playboy,
boy. today y'all gone admit
y'all like fat Black bitches.

and i look good.

you see that ass. that arch
that cellulite spilling
out across all six open tabs.
these stretch marks got stretch
marks. tiddies rolling over the side
of your screen. i know you like it.
i know, right?

LOOK AT THIS FAT BITCH

marvel at me. take it all in.
make   me   famous.
ain't no victim here. no shame.
just good lighting
and a fuckable face.

i'm a big glass of over your shit
and you looking thirsty   boy.

hidradenitis suppurativa pt. 1

ain't no tulip here. just a soft succulent. a little ugly cactus.
a perennial not for the faint. ribbed for your pleasure.
a little bruised but she taste sweet.

it's easier to pretend i don't hear my friends asking why
i didn't give my number to the girl eye-fucking me across
the bar than say

a woman getting familiar with my pussy is apocalyptic.
what could be worse than lying next to and all
up in something so beautiful and correct.

that no, this isn't what it looks like. i have this condition
right. and it makes these things. and like i be stressed
and i promise it's normal. it's okay. i'm okay. okay?

hidradenitis suppurativa pt. 2

so i have this thing right. like a condition. and it makes my
underarms look like a volcano is starting to form. or
reform. or just erupted. or like they were sculpted by a
makeup artist with a straight-to-netflix budget. and it
makes me feel so fucking less than. it's basically like boils
or cysts or really large pimples depending on the day. and
they bury themselves into my skin. like moles but they're
not moles. there is no cute metaphor for this thing that
makes me feel my worst. i get smaller ones on my breasts,
in between my thighs. i am crying. again. i get them
around my vagina and anus. this poem is written in pus
and salt. and this thing is so common. but we don't talk
about it. because it's ugly. and we are taught to bury our
ugly in lovers who have already seen us. cause i don't
know if finding a man who respects me is worth more than
the ones i've already shown my scars to. or explained my
scars to. or really carefully hidden them from him at 2 a.m.
in the dark or a sheet, enveloped by his smooth skin. i
don't know when or if i'll stop feeling ugly. all i know is i
have had this since i was sixteen. and i am still unsure how
to pronounce it. and i still haven't gotten good at hiding it
or not tearing up when a child stares too long on the
beach. i spent years not sitting on faces or being bent over
in the daylight. the thought of someone knowing would
stress me out so much that another one would grow. men
loved me. this girl who sucked dick without asking for
anything in return.

when non-nerd boys flirt with me they ask about superpowers

after nicole homer

volume 3

if i was to be honest. which i only do when it benefits me.
i'd choose replication.

volume 4

one to teach when i'm too tired of myself to leave my bed.
one to stare at the phone when he doesn't text back. one
to not give a fuck about him. one to learn to do my hair.
one to finally eat pussy. correctly. one to cry incessantly.
one to work out. one to perfect cosmopolitan's *ten easy
steps to get a man.* one to not obsess over the fact that
every girl in the pictures are ten sizes smaller. one to eat
whatever the fuck i want. one to watch my own back when
i am too drunk. or too alone. or too woman. one to watch
makeup tutorials. one to finally write that poem. one to
take a self-defense class. one to go to therapy. one to suck
his dick until he finds god in my mouth. one to brush it off
when he practices polytheism. one to not save his number
anyway. one to read the stack of books on my desk. on my
coffee table. on my nightstand. one to not be a
disappointment. one to call grandma more. one who is
called. one to laugh with a boy at the bar and not wonder
where the lie is.

an incomplete list:
of what to do when you're fucked

have another glass of pinot / write down all your favorite baby
names /

soleil. diem. saphira. bee.
assata. ivory. nori. margeaux.

burn them / not you / cradle you / another glass / it's only
somenumber a.m. / you have plenty of time / to sober up
before you teach / later / scroll through her facebook /
lament / over the pictures of her daughter / hate her
/ hate her / hate that you want / to hate her / send him a
nude / the one you spent twenty minutes trying to perfect
/ looking effortlessly / fuckable / berate yourself / for
being childish / cry / for her / cry for the her you cannot
have / have another glass / and another / and another /
get upset / with him / for not texting / back soon enough /
apologize / for the argument / he didn't know y'all had /
laugh / at what you thought were past pregnancy scares /
wish you could / hold her / you / be jealous / cause he's
holding her not you / title a poem / you won't start for a
week

titling

~~what to do when the guy you're fucking regularly cancels cause his *pseudo* girlfriend needs him~~
-
~~what to do when the guy you like cancels your regularly scheduled fucking appointment cause his girlfriend miscarries~~
-
~~an incomplete list: of ways to not let a man break you~~
-
~~an incomplete list: of things to do when the man you're fucking cancels your sex appointment cause his girlfriend(?) had a miscarriage~~

~~fuck him, cause he's not fucking you~~
-
~~an incomplete list: of things to do besides collapse into yourself when the man you're fucking raw cause you're probably infertile cancels your sex appointment cause his *maybe* girlfriend had a miscarriage~~

brenda's got three babies

we cannot un-etch the height ticks in the wall
we cannot un-grow our feet
we cannot reclaim our virginities
we cannot un-move out of her home

we cannot un-speak our *i hate yous*
we cannot retake our first steps
we cannot take back our father's features
we cannot un-love our first heartbreaks

we cannot regrow inside her
we cannot un-widen these hips
we cannot un-birth my niece
we cannot un-trauma the things we're still scared to tell

we cannot un-gray her hair
we cannot un-tie her tubes

my ob-gyn tells me i may not be able to have children

casually. in between a joke and her fingers inside.
something about scarred. something about trauma.
clinical. i do not laugh. it feels like she forgot to take a land
mine out. i refuse to cry, to be weak in front of another
woman. i am a small, brown train wreck driving home.

[sometimes] i wonder what it's like to be a woman and
have to give that news. if she ever feels less than.

i've cried in the pampers aisle of target. i used to fuck
unprotected, hoping it would end in a child that i had the
option to keep. i [want to] yell at tired moms. i am so
bitter to be an aunt. i take birth control to convince myself
it's a choice. my body feels like a sanctuary god or science
forgot to finish.

Go Go Gadget Hoe
@BlkRseKapri

Th only people I've seen excited about Harriet Tubman getting put on the 20$ bill are white allies.

10:18 AM · 13 May 15

harriettes

ladies, bitches, and tramps i got what you need, i got what
you want. step right up, step right up. hey you, yeah you
with the flat ass and thin lips, come a lil closer. dontcha
wanna be a bad bitch? dontcha wanna be a kylie, miley,
or katy? dontcha wan lowercase-black men to fawn all
over you? to throw dirt on they momma name so they can
rattle the spirit of mamie till just for a glimpse at a pink
nipple? giiiiirl, i got you. if you don't got it you can buy it.
ass, hair, followers. don't matter you can be a black
woman without all the welfare. so long as you got the
green. you ain't know? green buys anything black, boo. ay
little mama in the birkenstocks dontcha wanna slum it a
little before you accept that harvard legacy spot? wanna
know how the other side lives? just get you some nike
slides and you too can be a trap queen. we could make a
trade i'll give you the hot sauce in my bag if you give me
low-interest rates and lead-free water? you know i'm
kidding. i know you don't like hot sauce. are you tired of
your flat shapeless hair? take that up with white jesus. but
until then boxer braids are the new cornrows. plenty of
girls at the shop will whip up them wispy ass hairs for
double the price. always.

Go Go Gadget Hoe
@BlkRseKapri

Annual reminder of how to deal with Black face on Halloween

1. Carry pocket Baby powder
2. Remind them what color they're supposed to be

8:26 PM · 18 Oct 16

haiku for reparations

both these armrests mine
now. seat laid all the way back.
your comfort mine too.

micro

actually i don't understand martha, what do you mean
when you say i speak so well? oh, where did you expect
me to work mary-beth? i don't remember saying i lived on
the South Side muriel. are you telling me your hair doesn't
grow thirty inches overnight melanie? if i'm not like the
other ones, then who am i like melissa? do you follow
everyone around the store macy? when you say my
sentences connect do you mean like conjunctions molly?
well, where else could i have gotten my degree myrtle?
maggie i don't think i understand, what do you mean by
urban? are all kids inner city youth or just the Black ones
marilyn? so missy, beyoncé is your spirit animal . . . explain.
and why wouldn't you go back after you go Black mallory?
let me clarify when you say you wish you had skin like
mine do you mean scarred or sensitive maureen? do they
not have chicken where you're from magda? mackenzie
what's your name mean . . . no i mean back where your
family's from? i don't think i can be racist, i have a white
friend miranda, right?

an incomplete list:
of things to call white men

that call you nubian queen

-mayo daddy
-casper
-reparations
-glue stick
-plastic bag
-1&3
-coconut meat
-ben affleck
-pasty dictator
-dayglo
-saltless sultan
-woke
-pinky & the bran muffin
-bundt cake baby
-blocked
-cotton-picked
-officer
-sir

Go Go Gadget Hoe
@BlkRseKapri

I love telling #wipipo they clap on the 1 & 3 as an insult cause when they don't get it they prove my point.

2:21 PM · 25 Feb 16

36

a reading guide:
for white people reading my book

don't sister girl me or giiiiirl me or sis me or girlfriend me
or hey bitch me. or any other slang you think me and other
Black women call ourselves when you're not around.
making it to the end of the book does not open some
special key to nigga vernacular. i'm not your Black friend.
not your hero. this book isn't for you. it's a celebration of
my Blackness, my Queerness, my Hoeness, none of which
exists without the other. if you want to celebrate me, buy
me a shot or tell your cousins to stop asking if my wigs are
my real hair. now i know, that you know, not to say nigga.
but sometimes y'all act like you haven't seen the same
viral videos as me. you know, the ones where one of y'all
step outside y'all body to the wrong nigga and get y'all
whole ancestry knocked outta y'all. this book isn't a rap
song². something to get caught up in and *accidentally*
forget who you are. or where you are. if i see you reading
along mouthing the word nigga i will stop my whole ass set
to ask you why. embarrassing white folks and fuckboys is
my american pastime. this book isn't an invitation. i am
not your therapist or here to validate that one time you
stood up to your grandpa by telling him colored was
outdated. don't applaud yourselves. instead show a Black
woman you appreciate them. all we want is reparations
and to be left the fuck alone.

by you.

---

2 don't say nigga when you're rapping either

white daddy

my daddy white. well my real daddy not actually white. my
real daddy gone. not *gone* gone, not like left for cigarettes
in '93 gone. but gone like he don't ever show up when he
say he gone show up gone. my real daddy is a better
daddy to his new kids than he was to me, and that's okay. i
like them. my new daddy white. well he not *new* new.
he just not the original.

anyway my daddy white. white like ain't graduate high
school still went to university and law school white. white
like some of the shit he do is considered questionable and
not illegal cause he white. my daddy white and know he
white and don't pretend to be anything other than a
heterosexual cis white man with too much privilege and
not enough outlets. my white daddy use his privilege good.
and bad. my white daddy practice law in the hood. moved
his firm to the West Side. cause buses and redlining always
stopping his clients. where men who look like him only
come around with bad news or mormon jesus.

my white daddy love Black women. learned hard work and
unconditional giving from us. my white daddy love me.
love me most when i'm calling out whiteness and
systemic racism and his white ass for doing caucasian ass
shit.

my white daddy live in Southshore. he love South Side dive
bars and cheap property. is it gentrification if he don't
want white people to follow him? if his family Black? if he was
being priced out of the neighborhood he grew up in
cause a different type of white people discovered it? if he
buy property and move my Black ass family into it for an

affordable price? if he grew up Uptown hillbilly poor and
finally wanted something of his own?

my white daddy did not pay for my college. or my rent. or
my car. he won't let me drown but many times watched
me sink. he tough but honest. remind me often i'm not
safe in the same world as he is. i'm not promised anything
but the breath i just took. never let his family erase me or
my Black ass skin from holiday portraits or dinner tables.
was never a shield but taught me how to hold a sword.
how to spin a word. how to get pulled over and drive
away. he knew his privilege couldn't save me, so he used it
to teach me how to save myself.

# of wanting

let's skip
to where my partner
& i never stop
trying. lose
faith in doctors.
when her name
and learning
to pray
are the same words.

let's skip
to where all i can
do is write
poems that no longer
probably or
possibly. where her
absence is a nursery
turned home office.

let's skip
to where i accuse
my partner of wanting
more than i

can give.

purple

"i don't care if you're Black, white, green, or purple."
—ancient white proverb

i find it strange how these beings came to my planet
expecting to find themselves. as if the only thing i could
have been was a mirror. these bags of veins and alabaster
roughness, they sun don't even respect them. they won't
look me in my eye. won't shake my vines. won't learn
what's customary here. they expect i should know what
was never taught to me. they keep trying to convince me
they don't care what i look like. but i hear them, hear
them tell their friends i am lavender instead of raisin.
praise the lilac and periwinkle children they forced into
me. i see it, the slow erasure of my fig, my mulberry. i hear
them say *plum plague, plum magic, plum list, plum mail*
and i know that is not an accident. they offer me bleach
and name it peace. they teach my children to hate me in a
tongue i don't know. they tell me to never look back while
calling their history law. separate our families and call it a
statistic.

i miss watching the wild of my children spread without
fear. i miss the monuments dedicated to my darkness. i
miss facing my sun and saying good morning.

Juvenile Detention Center
Thursdays 5:30–7:00 p.m.

For the safety and Security of the ~~Facility~~ white people and its ~~occupants~~ niggas, the following is required of the ~~Employees, Contractors, Visitors,~~ niggas and ~~Volunteers~~ really well-intentioned white folks for entry (this list is ~~not~~ exhaust~~ive~~ing):

1. ~~Must provide proper identification upon entering the Facility.~~ who is you niggas?

2. Hair will be ~~clean, combed, and neatly trimmed or styled~~ eurocentric. ~~The hairstyle must be appropriate to the work setting and should not interfere with the work to be performed, create a safety hazard, or cause distractions in the workplace.~~ none of that nigga shit here

3. ~~Hair that extends below the collar~~ weave must be fastened and worn above the collar

4. Jewelry and other accessories will be appropriate for ~~the work setting~~ white comfort and not create a safety hazard or cause ~~other distractions~~ the whites to be uncomfortable.
> One small stud (non-dangling) earring per ear (no more than ¼″ diameter)[3].
> Necklace may be worn inside the shirt so it is not visible for uniformed employees.

6. Form-fitting ~~clothes including but not limited to Spandex, leggings, Jeggings, or Body Shirts are not~~

---

3 do y'all niggas know what a diameter is?

~~permitted.~~ women not permitted

7. ~~No slacks shall be worn inside boots.~~ we know you
smuggling shit niggas

8. ~~Tank-tops, cut-off and low-cut shirts are not allowed.~~
just don't have tiddies

10. ~~"Hoodies" are not permitted.~~ none of that hood nigga
shit here either

13. ~~Scarves and non-uniform hats are not permitted.~~ don't
bring your bonnet to work bitch

14. ~~Pre-Approved religious garments as long as they are~~
~~searched.~~ this here is christian-approved
slavery

dboy Black: a poem for briyae

your father is semiautomatic black. pound cake black. "call
me anything less than black and i'll fuck you up" black.
why go up north black? a bottle in one hand, rattle in the
other black. blunt tucked behind ear black. one of nine
black. my baby brother black. prison swole black. guttural
lullaby black. didn't really have a father around black.
couldn't wait to be yours black. no job black. still got
pampers black. mah-mah's boy black. stand alone black.
rapper like most black boys under six feet black. dread
head black. hates how pretty he is black. don't talk about
where he's been black. we don't ask black. loves you black.
will give you the world black. even if he has to shoot it up
Black.

for Colored boys who considered gangbanging when being Black was too much

I saw three little Black boys lying in a graveyard, I couldn't tell if they were playing or practicing.

—"rehearsal" by baba lukata

like all Black Chicago women i
have been preparing my womb to carry a stillborn.
a baby to grow, but not man. i
will bury him before i have finished
paying off his first hospital bills. i
have picked my daughter's name.
but can't bring myself to ready the words i'll
need for his tombstone. i
am trying to line my womb with kevlar.
like all Black Chicago women i
have been preparing my womb
to carry a Bigger Thomas,

my son is a name no one knows
in homicide tracker. or a blurb
in the tribune. a clutched purse, a whistle
in the wrong direction. a Black boy drowning.
there is no ticking, just the cock of the hammer banging
against my biological clock waiting for me to offer a new
sacrifice to these streets.

pink crayon

on the first day of first grade at a new school. a girl
punches me in the stomach while her older brother holds
me for allegedly stealing a pink crayon. at home my
mother asks how it felt. asks me if i ever want to feel that
way again. tells me to hit back. teaches me to not be a
victim.

in fourth grade a girl twice my size informs me we're going
to be fighting after school tomorrow. i replace all the
books in my bag with bricks. that same year a boy lifts up
my skirt and i uncrochet a braid from my head and choke
him outside the office. in fifth grade i dull a girl's face on
the asphalt months before cps changes all the
neighborhood parks to foam. sixth through eighth grade
my tongue is now as sharp as the screwdriver i keep in my
locker so folks don't challenge me. freshman year i sparta a girl
down half a flight of stairs, call her back up just to
kick her back down. i am all dagger mouth and bloody fist.
and i never ask questions later. sophomore through junior
year everyone at school understands i am in fact not the
one. on the block i drag a golf club with latin queens'
names etched into the head. at some point i crack three
different hockey sticks over three different boys' heads. i
see a person die for the first time. my only thought after is,
better him than me. my first year of college i begin
collecting swords. i keep switchblades in my pocket until
the desire to cut becomes stronger than a need for
survival.

how to title a poem about Ferguson, Chicago, Baltimore[4]

Black ~~boys disappearing is not magic, it's genocide~~

~~trying to be less martin, more Assata~~

~~i enjoy my father's white privilege~~

~~i fear we don't have the endurance of our grandparents~~

~~could i come back after the dogs?~~

Black ~~and college educated, now what?~~

~~i am not Michael Brown~~

~~Black as fuck in white spaces~~

~~grew up resenting white cousins for all the wrong reasons~~

~~i hope my brother dies a martyr not a thug~~

~~i will raise a~~ Black ~~son in Chicago~~

~~i am tired of rallying for~~ Black ~~men who turn around and call me angry~~

~~what's your badge number?~~

---

4 to the white editor who asked if i wanted to capitalize white since i had been capitalizing Black in my poem

Go Go Gadget Hoe
@BlkRseKapri

Y'all got a lot of "queen, shut up & take this trauma with a smile but also only fuck Black Men for the movement" ass "friends"

3:13 PM · 16 Aug 16

adverbs

for queen mo'nique

big girls need love ~~too~~.

you should have said no.
five years being
his joke.

you deserved more
than a finale.
a *finally*.

othered

it is the summer. i am at a 70th birthday party for an uncle
through marriage. in canada for the first time since i've
stopped coveting my white family's whiteness. and i am all
ears and very little mouth. and they laugh full laughs with
full bellies and it sounds like laugh tracks for shows i could
never relate to. and they joke about ~~my~~ the president. and
everything is so much lighter on this side of the border. i
mean isn't it all so funny. this megalomaniac so ridiculous.
so laughable. his tweets. and bans. and walls. and i wonder
what it must be like to not feel threatened all the time. to
know not only you but most almost everyone who looks
like you will make it out on the other side. on our drive to
canada for the first time in nineteen years we are stopped
by border patrol. but we are not Brown. i mean i am
brownish but not the Brown they are looking for. so we
are free to move on. i wonder if my white family who
drove from the comfort of their connecticut suburb was
also stopped. or did me and my mom darken our car just a
little too much this day. this is the part of the poem where
i am expected to invoke the holocaust and bans and
leaders with egos bigger than borders. where i remind or
pretend to remind my jewish family that they are only
a generation away from stars and ash. but i can't trust folks
who can only find empathy when facing a mirror. the *what
would you do if this was your mother or daughter* dudes,
the *us too* white folks.

instead i weaponize my silence. learn to fear my family.
begin to count the white women. and exits. learn to see
them like any other white folk on the street. on this day i
feel Blacker here than i have ever felt around my family.
and i know it is summer because at home someone is
murdered and forgotten in the same amount of time it
takes them to pass the basil lemonade.

quarter-life crisis

girl you been done had that. you was still in barrettes
and trainin bras. hoping ya first kiss ain't taste like doritos

and mountain dew. still not allowed to hear ya big mama
tell stories about your mama. still sittin at the small table

on thanksgivin. still gotta be in befo'e the streetlights
come on. still in kitten heels and dolla sto'e makeup. still

tryin to find your likeness in a disney princess with a
daddy. still askin permission to use the bathroom. still thinkin

you'd have your life together by 25. who told you Black
folks lived to 25? giiiiirl, you ain't know ... you a star.

a light that's been dead since the moment we saw you.

Black Queer Hoe

Black Queer Hoe shotguns pbrs on the red line before heading to a club where she can't afford the water bottles. she yells at her girls about the dick she just sucked across the slowdragging of the crowded train. she know people. finesses her way to the front so she don't have to wait in the cold. she sweats and sweats and throws it back until she forgets her tab is still open. she scared to be the only girl in the club in nikes. she wanna take her heels off but she scared to be called ratchet. she just requested cardi b. she used to care that niggas didn't want to dance with her. now she turn away niggas who grab or pull or spent the whole night holding up the wall. she pays the uber surcharge cause it's better than being followed home. she gives the address of two houses down in case the uber decides to follow her home. she stands naked in the kitchen drinking juice from the carton. she too drunk to remember if it's hers.

Black Queer Hoe makes sure her lesson for tomorrow is ready. checks both her emails and all three of her slack accounts before the room starts spinning. makes a note of all the work she didn't do tonight. of all the things she'll have to catch up on tomorrow. sends the "you alive bitch" text to her girls. thanks someone for keeping her alive. sets two alarms just in case. writes down the six lines of the poem that kept replaying in her head. takes her vitamins and birth control with the water waiting by her bed. she smokes a little so she doesn't think too long about all the ways in which she isn't successful. checks her credit and debit card balances. regrets nothing.

Go Go Gadget Hoe
@BlkRseKapri

Today is a day where I publicly twerk on things because I'm black, and mad and I want to.

12:17 PM · 15 Aug 14

my niggas & not niggas
thank you.

Brenda for pushing me out her pussy. Brendan. June.
Helen. Charlene. my ride or die Slutbucket Justice. Ricky.
Briyae. Jas & Erica & Kyra. my baby daddy, number one
down ass bitch Big Raychie Raych. Michilla & George.
Nate. José for 2006. Blaire. Danez for never letting a Bitch
get comfortable. Hieu. my partner Vince for constantly
waking up in the middle of the night to tell me to stop
working on this book in my half sleep. Jeremy. Shaun &
Sean. my whites, Aris & Molly & Adam & Ben Alfaro. Kevin
for editing a book in which he couldn't say half the words.
Cydney & Sydney. Demetrius. Franny. Fatimah. Jamila & Noname
& Joseph Chilliams for the albums this book was written to.
Qurissy & Reese. Niq. tOASTER! Kush. Emon. Matt Muse.
Dominique Chestand. Nicole Homer. Kane & Gaby. Rachel
McKibbens. Rachel Wiley. Siaara & Ajanae & Brittany.
Haymarket for believing in this book before you even saw
the poems. Rebecca & Mariah & Heather & Bayana & Alex.
Lauren. Kai. Kamaria. Eva. Dylan. Noa. Christina. Kara. Levi.
Charles. Madison. Ken. Sammy. Luis. Jalen. Sharita. Suubi.
Patricia. Keyante. Naudia. Sara. TLC. Tasia. Michaela. Amar.
Kee. Emily. Maceo & Nick. Mausi. Melo. Frsh. Saba. Cristela.
Squeak. Dimress. Walt. Rachel Claff. Elmo & Andrew. Krista
for always reminding me i'm messy boots. Avery R. Young.
Kaity & Anton. Delisa. Sllime. Confidence & Golden & Noor
& Princess. Samantha Irby for being the vulgar Bitch i
aspire to be. the Blackest of nerds Will & Lauren & Omar &
Jordan & Izetta. Nico. JP. Malcolm. Nayo & Miri.
Julian. Hanif & Eve with the bad takes. Pedro. Justice
& Chrysanthemum & Paul. Ydalmi. Mikey Haef. and
anyone who retweets my bullshit.

About Haymarket Books

Haymarket Books is a radical, independent, nonprofit book publisher based in Chicago. Our mission is to publish books that contribute to struggles for social and economic justice. We strive to make our books a vibrant and organic part of social movements and the education and development of a critical, engaged, international left.

We take inspiration and courage from our namesakes, the Haymarket martyrs, who gave their lives fighting for a better world. Their 1886 struggle for the eight-hour day—which gave us May Day, the international workers' holiday—reminds workers around the world that ordinary people can organize and struggle for their own liberation. These struggles continue today across the globe—struggles against oppression, exploitation, poverty, and war.

Since our founding in 2001, Haymarket Books has published more than five hundred titles. Radically independent, we seek to drive a wedge into the risk-averse world of corporate book publishing. Our authors include Noam Chomsky, Arundhati Roy, Rebecca Solnit, Angela Y. Davis, Howard Zinn, Amy Goodman, Wallace Shawn, Mike Davis, Winona LaDuke, Ilan Pappé, Richard Wolff, Dave Zirin, Keeanga-Yamahtta Taylor, Nick Turse, Dahr Jamail, David Barsamian, Elizabeth Laird, Amira Hass, Mark Steel, Avi Lewis, Naomi Klein, and Neil Davidson. We are also the trade publishers of the acclaimed Historical Materialism Book Series and of Dispatch Books.

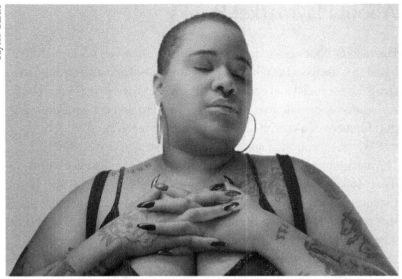

Britteney Black Rose Kapri is a poet, teaching artist, petty enthusiast, and Slytherin from Chicago. Currently, she is an alumna turned Teaching Artist Fellow at Young Chicago Authors. She is a staff member of Black Nerd Problems and Pink Door Women's Writing Retreat. Her first chapbook titled *Winona and Winthrop* was published in June of 2014 through New School Poetics. She has also been published in *The Break-Beat Poets* volumes one and two, *Poetry Magazine*, *Vinyl*, *Day One*, *Seven Scribes*, the *Offing*, *Kinfolks Quarterly*, and her number has appeared on many dive bar bathroom walls. She is a 2015 Rona Jaffe Writers Award Recipient. You can probably find her on Twitter talking shit about all the things you love, in a classroom talking shit about your kids, or on a barstool just talking shit.

CPSIA information can be obtained
at www.ICGtesting.com
Printed in the USA
JSHW051802070323
38613JS00004B/4